Life Cycles

Broad Bean

Louise Spilsbury

Raintree

LEARNING
RESOURCES
◇+□ *for* □+◇
EDUCATION
your schools library service

www.raintreepublishers.co.uk

Visit our website to find out more information about **Raintree** books.

To order:

☎ Phone 44 (0) 1865 888112

▤ Send a fax to 44 (0) 1865 314091

▢ Visit the Raintree Bookshop at **raintreepublishers.co.uk** to browse our catalogue and order online.

First published in Great Britain by Raintree, Halley Court, Jordan Hill, Oxford OX2 8EJ, part of Harcourt Education.
Raintree is a registered trademark of Harcourt Education Ltd.

Editorial: Charlotte Guillain and Diyan Leake
Design: Michelle Lisseter
Picture Research: Maria Joannou and Debra Weatherley
Production: Lorraine Hicks

Originated by Dot Gradations
Printed and bound in China by South China Printing Company

10 digit ISBN 1 844 21249 1 (hardback)
13 digit ISBN 978 1 844 21249 1 (hardback)
07 06 05 04
10 9 8 7 6 5 4 3 2
10 digit ISBN 1 844 21254 8 (paperback)
13 digit ISBN 978 1 844 21254 5 (paperback)
08
10 9 8 7 6 5 4

British Library Cataloguing in Publication Data
Spilsbury, Louise
Broad bean
571.8'2374
A full catalogue record for this book is available from the British Library.

Acknowledgements
The publishers would like to thank the following for permission to reproduce photographs: Anthony Blake p. 22; Chris Honeywell p. 17; Corbis pp. 5 (Michael Boys), 7 (Robert Maass); Garden Picture Library pp. 13 (Howard Rice), 19 (Steven Wooster); Holt Studios pp. 12 (Nigel Cattlin), 18 (Inga Spence), 23 (pod, Inga Spence); Nature Picture Library pp. 15 (John B. Free), 16 (Premaphotos), 23 (nectar, John B. Free; pollen, Premaphotos); Oxford Scientific Films pp. 6, 8, 9, 10, 11, 23 (root, seed, shoot), back cover; Photo Horticultural pp. 4 (Michael & Lois Warren), 14; The Garden Picture pp. 20, 21 (David Askham)

Cover photograph of broad beans, reproduced with permission of FLPA (Richard Becker)

Every effort has been made to contact copyright holders of any material reproduced in this book. Any omissions will be rectified in subsequent printings if notice is given to the publishers.

Contents

Some words are shown in bold, **like this**. They are explained in the glossary on page 23.

What is a broad bean?

Broad beans are a kind of **seed**.

They grow inside a **pod**.

We can cook broad beans and
eat them.

Where do broad beans grow?

Broad beans grow on plants.

Broad bean plants start life
as a **seed**.

People put bean seeds in soil.

The seeds need water to help
them grow.

How do bean plants grow?

First a **root** grows.

It grows out of the **seed** and down into the soil.

Next a **shoot** starts to grow.

The shoot grows up.

What do roots and shoots do?

The **shoot** grows up out of the soil.

It grows into the light.

The **root** grows lots of little roots.

They suck up water for the plant.

When do leaves and flowers grow?

After 6 weeks leaves begin to open on the young bean plant.

The leaves are dark green.

After 12 weeks flowers start
to grow.

What are the flowers like?

The flowers are black and white.

They look like little butterflies.

Bees visit the flowers.

They drink a sweet juice called **nectar** from inside the flowers.

How do bees help beans grow?

Pollen from the flower sticks to the bee.

Pollen looks like yellow dust.

The pollen rubs off on a different flower.

The pollen starts a bean growing in the flower.

How do beans grow?

The flowers die and drop off the plants.

The beans grow inside **pods**.

The pods keep the beans safe.

Inside the pods it is soft and damp.

When are beans ready to eat?

In summer the beans and **pods** are big and long.

It is time to pick and eat the beans.

In autumn the bean plant goes
brown and dies.

You can use the brown beans to
grow new plants.

Broad bean map

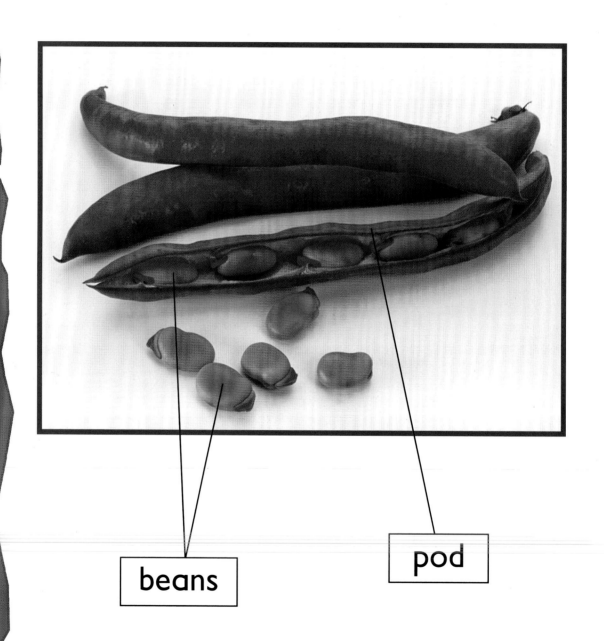

beans

pod

Glossary

 nectar sweet juice in the centre of a flower

 pod part of a plant that beans grow in

 **pollen** yellow dust in flowers

 **root** part of a plant that grows under the ground. It takes in water for a plant.

 **seed** new plants grow from seeds. Beans are a kind of seed.

 **shoot** the first stem and leaves of a new plant

Index